# Out of Gaza
## New Palestinian Poetry

# Out of Gaza
## New Palestinian Poetry

Edited by Atef Alshaer
and Alan Morrison

**Smoke STACK BOOKS**

Smokestack Books
School Farm
Nether Silton
Thirsk
North Yorkshire
YO7 2JZ
e-mail: info@smokestack-books.co.uk
www.smokestack-books.co.uk

Poems copyright
the authors, 2024.
All rights reserved.

ISBN 9781739473457

Smokestack Books
is represented
by Inpress Ltd

# Contents

| | |
|---|---|
| Introduction | 11 |

**Ali Abukhattab**
| | |
|---|---|
| Empty | 19 |
| why can't I write? | 20 |
| Waiting for Godot Again | 21 |
| Variations on Genesis | 22 |
| Trilogy for the Sea | 24 |
| Discourse of I\You | 25 |

**Refaat Alareer**
| | |
|---|---|
| If I must die | 26 |
| I am You | 27 |

**Hala Alyan**
| | |
|---|---|
| Tattler | 30 |
| Heirloom | 32 |
| Naturalised | 33 |
| I don't mean to hate the sparrows | 35 |

**Farid Bitar**
| | |
|---|---|
| Unexplained misery | 38 |
| The Journalist | 39 |
| Child of Gaza | 40 |

**Tariq Luthun**
| | |
|---|---|
| The Summer My Cousin Went Missing | 41 |
| We Already Know This | 42 |
| Al-Bahr | 43 |
| For Those We Left Behind | 45 |
| Sermon (For Those Who Survive) | 46 |
| I Go to the Backyard to Pick Mint Leaves for My Mother | 47 |

**Marwan Makhoul**
Portrait of the People of Gaza                              48
New Gaza                                                    50
Hello Beit Hanoun                                           53
Lines Without a Home                                        55

**Mohammed Mousa**
In a country that doesn't need me,                          59
Gaza children play in cemeteries                            62
I don't want my memories to grow old on foreign soil        63
Salted Wounds                                               64
I can't keep up with the rhythm of war                      65
Three military vehicles drive by                            66
Hungry Gaza Skies                                           67
They ask me who I am                                        68

**Hiba Abu Nada**
We are in the heights now                                   69
Good night, Gaza                                            70

**Naomi Shihab Nye**
Green Shirt                                                 71
Before I Was a Gazan                                        72
Moon Over Gaza                                              73

**Samah Sabawi**
Questions the media should ask the people of Gaza           74

**Sara M. Saleh**
Say Free Palestine                                          76
The Business of Occupation Bingo                            77
There are no colonisers in this poem                        78
The Purging                                                 79

**Deema K. Shehabi**
Gaza Renga                                                  80
Light in the Orchard                                        82
Of Harvest and Flight                                       83
Blue                                                        86

**Dareen Tatour**
A moment before death ... 88
The general, my brother and me ... 90
The child and the sea ... 92
When Gaza was killed ... 93
I will not die ... 94

**Mosab Abu Toha**
What is Home? ... 95

**Lena Khalaf Tuffaha**
Grisaille ... 96
Pianissimo ... 97
The State of – ... 98
Abjadarian in Autumn ... 99

Acknowledgements ... 101
Biographies ... 103

# Introduction

Poetry at times of grave violence and danger as that experienced by the 2.3 million living in Gaza is something akin to the terrible impossible in all our dreams. But the higher calling of humanity makes poetry a duty, a duty to register pain and communion between and with the oppressed, with those whose very lives are under severe risk. In this case, poetry is a duty because it records the last stand of the soul as it stares death and destruction in the face, such keenness for the human voice to survive, and live long after humanity failed to preserve life and after all the cries for justice were not heeded. Guns, bombs, rockets, and other tools of killing and destruction are deafening methods of silencing and robbing people of their humanity. Poetry, on the other hand, this poor companion of the oppressed and anybody with a living soul, can serve as a humanising force, a repository of meaning and remembrance to lives lost and landscapes destroyed. Hence Palestinians have been remarkable keepers of the human spirit as it uncovers its endangered self through poetry, song, and literature. Palestinians hang on to poetry, live by it, and breathe it as their witness and shelter from oblivion and loss, the loss of the body, the house, and the landscape of their homeland that they so cherish and die for.

Poetry can never replace the physical presence of humanity in the form of flesh and spirit, of personality, but it can speak for their absence. In this speaking, there is the tenderest call for the corresponding and living spirits of other human beings to listen and respond. To respond is to imagine, and to imagine is to exist, and to exist is to reclaim and share one's humanity with others in the form of words, images, and art. Art can galvanise the shared spirit of humanity to empathise, reject and resist oppression. In this vein, I read and see Palestinian poetry and its history. I recall one of the earliest Palestinian poets, Ibrahim Tauqan (1905–1945), whose iconic portrayal of the Palestinians, whether freedom fighters or ordinary people, resonates beyond its time and space in the 1930s under the British Mandate (1921–1948). This is when Palestinian poetry started to emerge and bear witness to lives under severe risk and a homeland under threat of ethnic cleansing and destruction. This terrible reality came to materialise in 1948 when Israel was established at the expense of the Palestinians, whose villages and towns were levelled, and whose people were dispossessed and made homeless.

> Do not ask about his wellbeing
> He clasps his soul in his hand.
> His stitches a dress from his worries
> a coffin from his pillow.

This poetry does not represent 'recollection in tranquillity' as William Wordsworth defined poetry. Rather, it emanates from a place of urgency and struggle to stay and record life amidst acts of destruction, in this case by the advancing Zionist militias whose takeover of Palestine in 1948 was paved by the British. It speaks of the Palestinian human being, who is forced to carry his soul in his hands and to stitch a coffin from his pillow. There is no tranquillity, which stable living can bring forth. Palestinian poetry developed and metastasised so that in the 1960s and 70s, and later, Palestinian poets, such as Mahmoud Darwish, Samih al-Qassim, Fadwa Tauqan and Mu'in Bessiso, came to poeticise Palestinian lives and held them as mirrors to conditions of statelessness, refugee-hood, struggle, suffering, and death. Yet, it bears mentioning that Palestinian poetry is not all gloom and doom, despite the gloominess besetting Palestinian lives. If Palestinian poetry has been a witness, it's been a witness to a people with struggling hearts and visionary minds. It is a poetry populated with beauty, humanity, and hope, notwithstanding the brokenness of humanity that marred Palestinian life and continues to undermine its very viability.

In this context, Gaza is at the heart of the Palestinian landscape of poetry. Historically, Gaza served as a significant crossing between the two vast continents of Asia and Africa. Gaza earned a historical significance as a seat of ancient, medieval and modern civilisations, from the Pharaohs of Egypt to the Greek, Roman, Islamic, Ottoman, and British. Gaza is a small enclave of land, carved from historical Palestine, sitting over 363 kilometres, representing under 2% of historic Palestine. It was occupied by Israel in 1967. It has been crowded with Palestinian refugees from historic Palestine and has increasingly been made destitute and beyond hope of wellbeing or prosperity. Dominated and besieged by sea, land, and air by the Israeli occupation, its oppression has been left to fester, particularly over the last seventeen years. Israel bombed and attacked Gaza many times over this period, killing thousands of Palestinians and rendering life in the small strip wanting. On 7th October 2023, Hamas fighters breached the heavily fortified borders and attacked Israeli military installations along the borders with Gaza, and Israeli civilian communities, not far from the borders. Literally the following day, the Israeli bombardment of Gaza began, inflicting death and destruction, so often indiscriminately.

At the time of writing, more than 30,000 Gazans, mostly civilians, including children (over 8,000 and counting) and women. This is a staggering number of deaths, alongside the homes and civilian infrastructures that Israel had deliberately destroyed Gaza has been essentially made uninhabitable, and people are hanging by a thread to survive daily, while the tally of death and destruction climbs by the hour. Each of the deaths possesses a face and soul, and therefore the very essence of poetry. In certain cases, there is poetry in the form of concrete words that record the danger and death. Many Palestinian poets of Gaza, women, and men, have perished in this terrible deployment of death by the Israeli weaponry, mostly supplied and supported by the US and other western nations. As have so many Palestinian intellectuals and thinkers, including doctors, scientists, journalists, and teachers. The cry of poetry for justice and remembrance in this case is real. It is the last stand of the soul, as lives become at risk of death.

What can poets say and record at such moments? This is what this collection documents. It provides examples of poems from Gaza, and about Gaza, and Palestine. The collection stands as a witness to terrible times when Palestinians experience death in their thousands in Gaza, and the West Bank, the territories most connected with Palestinian nationalism and prospective statehood. The collection includes poems by poets who were killed by Israeli attacks in Gaza, including the university Professor and writer Rifat Al-'Ar'eer, and the poet and novelist Hiba Abu Nida. Both wrote poems and posted them on social media just a little while before they were killed by Israel in Gaza. Their poems are an extraordinary manifestation of souls that testify to their humanity and their stand as endangered witnesses against deadly oppression that knows no boundaries and is criminal in its extremes that we see in Gaza. Their poetry continues the tradition of testimony to Palestinian culture, nationhood, and humanity, which have all been severely targeted by Israel and its imperial Western backers. We read their desires, their tribulations, their characters, their fears, their hopes, and their undying belief in the justice and humanity of the Palestinian struggle, as a struggle for liberation from a criminal occupation that robs them of land and dignity.

Writing about poems grieving the ongoing genocide of Gaza is painful. As it continues, we are dealing with death upon death; pain piles up and trauma festers in the soul. Tariq Luthun draws the picture poignantly in one of the poems in this anthology: 'child upon child goes, and some's mother/is no longer a mother'. The loss of family members and the catastrophic conditions in Gaza are present in Lena Khalaf Tuffaha's poem, which echoes Luthun's. Such loss is enormous and evokes images of unrelenting suffering:

> Our children study these images,
> their cousins' corpses lightfast,
> their cries passing through
> networks of metal and verdigris,
> calling for water and father and air.

Such images of suffering, encapsulated in family loss and shortages in basic human needs, such as water and food, make it difficult to read the poem, but poetry is at the most noble levels an intimate communion with human suffering. Suffering remembers nostalgia for better times in the past and desperately so for the future, as Tariq movingly registers the hope when the death and destruction stop:

> ...a chase, a hunt, a honey, a home
> for the tea to settle; a haven
> for us to return to.

The poet is endowed with hope which the very act of poetry writing engenders. This hope is tragically present in the poem of the martyr Hiba Abu Nada, written shortly before her tragic killing:

> ...new families without pain or sadness,
> journalists taking pictures of heaven
> writing about the eternal love.
> All, all of them are from Gaza.
> There is a new Gaza in heaven
> without siege
> taking shape now.

This poem serves as a window into an unprecedented state of death and destruction in Palestine in terms of scale and consequences that poets lament and register with poignancy, dignity, and vision. This anthology is in some way a document of images, shot with poignant words, of love, solidarity, and suffering humanity.

This is not a poetry that can be underestimated or forgotten. Its merit stems from its urgency as witness to danger experienced by fellow human beings, whose only sin has been to be born in an occupied country. This poetry is collective in its grief, and serious in its demand for attention and solidarity. The individual voice is imbued with the collective predicament of Palestine and the Palestinians, against whom the Israeli occupation uses extreme methods of destruction to make them invisible, besmirch their humanity and attempt to wipe their entire culture from the map. Palestinians as colonised and oppressed people have refused to submit to such inhumanity unleashed against them, resorting to poetry to register their presence, humanity, and talent. Gaza is the apex that they have experienced in terms of the imposition of death and destruction by the Israeli occupation against them. Their poetry draws on a wide variety of references, registering feelings, fears, memories, and hopes, including from elements of their Arab and Islamic cultures, and their own experiences as human beings subjected, along with their families and communities, to severe pain and persecution.

The poetry in this collection emphasises the humanity of Palestinians and their remarkable spirit for survival in the face of repeated acts of dehumanisation, oppression, and disfiguration by the Israeli occupation. Israel as a settler colony, built on the ruins of Palestinian homes and lives, has been adept at undermining Palestinians and their national struggle. It uses the sheer weight of its power, which includes military, media, and economic methods, to subject the Palestinians to its racist and destructive policies. Palestinian poetry, including from within Gaza and outside it, but engaging with the plight of Gaza and the Palestinians more widely, stands as voices of resistance, remembrance, and commemoration of lives lost and humanity repeatedly targeted.

This collection is but one example of a response to an urgent situation where the Palestinians in Gaza struggle for their very survival, while many of them are killed by Israel daily. The people of Gaza and Palestine are living through extreme acts of colonial destruction, which reminds one of previous attempts by settler colonial powers to annihilate native lives and cultures, as in Algeria and much of Africa and elsewhere. Through their faith in poetry and language, the poets of Gaza and Palestine remind us that their souls are sacred, and they are heirs of rich cultures. They must be remembered and seen as makers of life and humanity amidst extreme conditions.

**Atef Alshaer**

As this anthology testifies, many Palestinian poets have been killed in the continuing Israeli bombardment of the Gaza Strip, two of them included here, Refaat Alareer and Hiba Abu Nada – in the case of Refaat Alareer (6 December 2023), a deliberate targeting of him and his family by an IDF 'surgical bomb' struck at their apartment (Euro-Med Monitor). Such targeting of poets, scholars, academics, journalists, universities and places of worship (and simultaneous pogroms in the West Bank) all emphasize how, in addition to the unconscionable ethnic cleansing of the Palestinian people, the Netanyahu regime is attempting to wipe out Palestinian culture altogether – these are all classic aspects to genocide and have informed the ICJ's provisional ruling that South Africa's genocide case against Israel is 'plausible' (26 January 2024). This 'cultural genocide' means it is becoming ever more imperative for contemporary Palestinian poets and writers to document their witness to a second Nakba, and I am humbled to have been commissioned to assist in giving some of them the platform of this anthology through which to do so. It is significant that most of the contributors to this anthology are poets of the Palestinian diaspora who, by dint of residing in other countries (the United States, Canada, Australia, Norway and Egypt among them), are better placed than their Gazan contemporaries to be able to write about the ongoing Palestinian catastrophe. The notable exception in this book is Mosab Abu Toha, a survivor of Gaza, who was able to eventually escape the Strip after having been detained by the IDF during which time he was beaten, and whose release came about due to mounting international pressure; visibly in discomfort, he recounted his experience on the 21 November edition of *Democracy Now*.

**Alan Morrison**

# Ali Abukhattab

## Empty

The wind has its logic...
And you walk against the saltiness of time.
The place's smell croaks in you.
You spin your death by hands made up of holes.
You stick to the wind's hissing
Your self burnt on the flame of fragmentation
You create your ceremonies
Mixing the tears by the phantom foam
Your crushed myth rises from the poem hell
      Go up
          Go up
              Go up
Do not stop on the tip of chant
      I see them approaching from your echo
      I see them slipping from the cough attendants
Escape,
Follow the prophecy of wind

## why can't I write?

(1)
Because I'm stronger than an idea,
        And weaker than a language
(2)
Because I'm bigger than an illusion
        And smaller than a fact
(3)
Because I'm clearer than a nothingness
        And more mysterious than an existence.

## Waiting for Godot Again

I, at the first of distance, am waiting for him.
As a defeated prophet
The time scorpions are biting me
The wild age words are stoning me
The weakness is spreading into the rocks
I said he must come
But they left me
I waited till the dates evaporated
.. ... .. ... .
Nothing came except death.

# Variations on Genesis

(1)
In the beginning was the desire,
Was going around the nowhere,
Embracing the illusion,
So, it died as smoke.
When it ecstasised by fact light
It got lost in the silence of time.

(2)
In the beginning was the bomb,
God lighted its fuse,
So he dispersed as fragment.

(3)
In the beginning the apple was in the hand of Eve
And Cain's hand carried the knife
Abel's neck bled
When Adam had eaten the apple.

(4)
In the beginning was the crime;
It's the first and the last.
And was the spite;
It's the visible
And the hidden.

---

*Note: 'The first', 'the last', 'the visible' and 'the hidden' are names for God in Islam.*

(5)
In the beginning God wrote his autobiography
On the kept sheet
And when destiny bewildered us
We said; Good and peace are from God
      And evil and war are from the Devil

(6)
Excuse for the Devil

# Trilogy for the Sea

(1)
The narcissus's desire
Draws abstraction for the finite
Picks, from my smell, an ink
And I still write.

(2)
A violet rests steep
In this green storm
My pen swims like the jellyfish
My face is a jutting rock
My mouth is moss
And I still speak.

(3)
The coast is the start of the flock
The fish fished the sea colour
My eyes smell the cloud
And I still look.

# Discourse of I\You

I am the shadow inflammation
You are the darkness drizzle
I am the mirror's masturbation
You are the mud labyrinth
I am the tail fire
You are a poem of dusk
I stumble in the dream lanes
You have erotic dreams in barbarian climate
I stare in cursed behind
You ride the trembling breath
I ride the horse of chaos
You fall at a distance of two seconds from my soul
I stand up leaned on the space
You rest on the branches of air
I am a soul that practices its secret habit
You are a body which exercises ceremonies of desolation
My nerves are the memory of dust
You act the tragedy of a mote
I build the kingdom of crying
You vibrate in memory's bow
I am killed by the clearness
You suffer the ambiguous coldness.

# Refaat Alareer

## If I must die

If I must die,
you must live
to tell my story
to sell my things
to buy a piece of cloth
and some strings,
(make it white with a long tail)
so that a child, somewhere in Gaza
while looking heaven in the eye
awaiting his dad who left in a blaze –
and bid no one farewell
not even to his flesh
not even to himself –
sees the kite, my kite you made, flying up above
and thinks for a moment an angel is there
bringing back love
If I must die
let it bring hope
let it be a tale

# I am You

...Look in the mirror:
The horror, the horror!
The butt of your M-16 on my cheekbone
The yellow patch it left
The bullet-shaped scar expanding
Like a swastika,
Snaking across my face,
The heartache flowing
Out of my eyes dripping
Out of my nostrils piercing
My ears flooding
The place.
Like it did to you
70 years ago
Or so.
I am just you.
I am your past haunting
Your present and your future.
I strive like you did.
I fight like you did.
I resist like you resisted
And for a moment,
I'd take your tenacity
As a model,
Were you not holding
The barrel of the gun
Between my bleeding
Eyes.
...The very same gun
The very same bullet
That had killed your Mom
And killed your Dad
Is being used,

Against me,
By you.
Mark this bullet and mark in your gun.
If you sniff it, it has your and my blood.
It has my present and your past.
It has my present.
It has your future.
That's why we are twins,
Same life track
Same weapon
Same suffering
Same facial expressions drawn
On the face of the killer,
Same everything
Except that in your case
The victim has evolved, backward,
Into a victimizer.
I tell you.
I am you.
Except that I am not the you of now.
I do not hate you.
I want to help you stop hating
And killing me.
I tell you:
The noise of your machine gun
Renders you deaf
The smell of the powder
Beats that of my blood.
The sparks disfigure
My facial expressions.
Would you stop shooting?
For a moment?
Would you?
All you have to do
Is close your eyes
(Seeing these days
Blinds our hearts.)

Close your eyes, tightly
So that you can see
In your mind's eye.
*Then look into the mirror.*
*One. Two.*
*I am you.*
*I am your past.*
*And killing me,*
*You kill you.*

# Hala Alyan

## Tattler

In Europe an ex-lover left me to eat alone. A shy bushboy brought me an extra macaroon, pink in his hand. His eyes dart around before he mutters in Arabic, *Ana min Iraq.*

◊

the bar where a man said

*I'll fuck the Arab out of you*

the news report where a man said

*O Allah my daughter's daughter*

(a braid without a head to swing from)

◊

I tell the bushboy I'm sorry, sorry, sorry. His eyes the colour of cognac.

We shred the cocktail napkins into a pile of white. He says when the Americans came to his town, they *didn't care who*, they asked the women to stay in their houses, *even when I say I am a good man,* they still shot at the neighbourhood trees. His favourite birds, *the chattering ones*, fell from the branches.

*Like this*, he says. The white fluttering from his fingers.

◊

birdsong:

the things that wash up on the shore
panties and televisions
jukeboxes and toddlers

◊

I am honouring my script. I remove my shoes carefully. I let the Israeli soldier run her fingers through my hair for a long time, until it feels more like love than anything else, and for a moment I wonder what she'd do if I shut my eyes, started singing until it was over. She follows every curl. She smiles thinly when I tell her not to worry, she couldn't brush it if she tried. Don't you understand, I want to say.

◊

Wasp like my husband's father. The right spoon, salty gimlets, a lake house in Maine. Wasp like plane, nosedive.

◊

Don't you understand, my hair *is* the army.

◊

Two soldiers at the border. *You can throw a rock if you want.*

One of them pretends to read my passport.

He wants to remove my belt. He wants to know why I'm here.

# Heirloom

My grandfather learned Hebrew *because they learn Arabic.* I am the daughter of Nafez. The granddaughter of Mohammed.

The granddaughter of Salim.

I usher in each dream with Quran. Yes, Mama, I'm reading the suras again. But I don't fast. I don't kneel.

*There's no desert without fire.*

The desert's bronze capillaries from the airplane. In a marbled room I played poker with a soldier. Ex-soldier, he reminded me.

*Tie up your camels and trust in Allah.*

*The bald woman boasts of her niece's hair.*
I make you sing for our houseguests.

*The carpenter's door is falling apart.*

There are men who sing to keep the sky from collapsing like a blue tent.

In the settlements I became Shoshanna. I gave Shoshanna something to love. The shirtless teenage boys with rifles, the swimming pools blue as blue.

The abandoned buildings had black graffiti in Hebrew I couldn't read. Shoshanna asked what it meant, memorised *we will come back you cannot keep us out we will return this is ours.*

# Naturalised

Can I pull the land from me like a cork?
I leak all over brunch. My father never learned to swim.
I've already said too much.
Look, the marigolds are coming in. Look, the cuties
are watching Vice again. Gloss and soundbites.
They like to understand. They like to play devil's advocate.
My father plays soccer. It's so hot in Gaza.
No place for a child's braid. Under
that hospital elevator. When this is over.
When this is over there is no over but quiet.
Coworkers will congratulate me on the ceasefire
and I will stretch my teeth into a country.
As though I don't take Al Jazeera to the bath.
As though I don't pray in broken Arabic.
It's okay. They like me. They like me in a museum.
They like me when I spit my father from my mouth.
There's a whistle. There's a missile fist-bumping the earth.
I draw a shampoo map on the shower curtain.
I break a Klonopin with my teeth and swim.
The newspaper says truce and C-Mart
is selling pomegranate seeds again. Dumb metaphor.
I've ruined the dinner party. I was given a life. Is it frivolous?
Sundays are tarot days. Tuesdays are for tacos.
There's a leak in the bathroom and I get it fixed
in thirty minutes flat. All that spare water.
All those numbers on the side of the screen.
Here's your math. Here's your hot take.
That number isn't a number.
That number is a first word, a nickname, a birthday song in June.

I shouldn't have to tell you that. Here's your testimony,
here's your beach vacation. Imagine:
I stop running when I'm tired. Imagine:
There's still the month of June. Tell me,
what op-ed will grant the dead their dying?
What editor? What red line? What pocket?
What earth. What shake. What silence.

# I don't mean to hate the sparrows

*I heard you in the other room asking your mother, 'Mama, am I a Palestinian?' When she answered 'Yes' a heavy silence fell on the whole house. It was as if something hanging over our heads had fallen, its noise exploding, then – silence.*

        Ghassan Kanafani, in a letter to his son Fayez


I don't mean to hate the sparrows.
I don't mean to close my eyes and see fire, a flood of concrete,
leaflets the size of grotesque snow.
I don't mean to rehearse evacuation that isn't mine:
from the grocery store to the house, from the house to the river,
from the river to the airport. Here are the rules.
There is a road and it's gone now.
There is a sea and you can't drink its water.
How far can you carry a toddler? A middle-aged dog?
How far can you go in sixty-five seconds? Eleven?
If you have a favourite flower, now's the time to redact it.
If you have a mother, now's the time to move her to the basement.
If you don't have a basement?
I don't mean to profit from this poem but I do.
I don't mean to say I but I do. Here are the rules.
The rules are redacted.
[  ] is [    ].
[  ] is a red herring.
[  ] is a billboard with 583 names.
Here are the rules.
I had a grandmother once.
She had a memory once.
It spoiled like milk.

On the phone, she'd ask me about my son, if he was fussy,
if he was eating solids yet.
She'd ask if he was living up to his name.
I said yes. I always said yes. I asked for his name and it was
[    ].
I dreamt of her saying:
[    ]
[    ]
[    ].
How deep in the earth can you burrow with your four hearts?
Here are the rules:
There is no bomb shelter. There is no ship.
You can leave. Why aren't you leaving?
You can resist. Why aren't you resisting?
On the phone, my grandmother would call me her heart.
Her soul. Her two God-given eyes.
She'd ask if I wanted to visit Palestine again.
I never brought her back any soil, but she liked one story,
so I'd tell it again, about the man I met at the
bus station, a stranger until he spoke Arabic,
calling me sister and daughter and sister and I told her how
he skipped work and drove me past the
gardens to the highest point and we waved to Beirut.
I waved to her, and later she said she was waving back.
Never mind her balcony faced the wrong direction.
Never mind the sea a terrible blue.
Never mind there never was a son. Here are the rules:
If you say Gaza you must say [       ].
If you say [    ] you must say [    ].
Here are the rules.
If there is a microphone do not sing into it.
If there is a camera do not look it in the eye.
Here are the rules.
You can't redact a name once it's been spoken.
If you say [    ] you must say [       ].
If you say Gaza, you must say Gaza.
If you look, you must look until there is no looking left to do.

Here are the rules. Here's my mother-given name,
    here's my small life.
It is no more than any other. Here's my grandmother,
    dead for five years.
She's speaking again. She calls when I'm not expecting.
*Keef ibnik*, she says. *Where is he now? Let me say hello.*
What could I say back? *He's good*, I tell her.
I pretend to call a child from the other room.
I pretend to hear the sea from here. I wave back.
    Here are the rules:
We bear what we bear until we can't anymore.
We invent what we can't stand grieving.
The sun sets on Gaza. The sun rises on Gaza.
On your [     ].
On your blue pencils.
On your God-given eyes.
*He's good*, I tell her. *He's good.*
*He's crawling. Mashallah, mashallah.*
Together, we praise the sea and the son.
Together, we praise how much he's grown.

# Farid Bitar

## Unexplained misery

The wars of Palestine are never ending
Insisting to never leave anytime
As the many years pass
As I get older than a stone
As the millions of olive trees uprooted

The wars keep coming back with vengeance
My nightmare keeps revisiting
I run away from it, seeking refuge in the woods
With a majestic lake greeting me camping
And the fog lifting at sunrise
Gaza keeps erupting with bunker bombs

I keep screaming, for the bombs to stop dropping
I keep praying for a miracle
I keep thinking this is a bad dream
And when I awake
Everything
From the previous day
Is just the same.

# The Journalist

At the crack of dawn
Rushing to watch the update on Gaza
A friend shares a post from Al Jazeera
A journalist describing chilling details
Wearing a bullet proof vest with
PRESS plastered on his chest
Stone-faced Momen Al-Sharafi
Narrating about his 21 family members
All perished from an airstrike dropping barrel bombs
His mother sending a last message
Telling him how much she missed not seeing him

Naming all of them one by one
Stone-faced to the end of the report
Brave souled survivor of an atrocity
My tears falling like a bloody river
Over his misery
Reminding me of my own family
That perished from the napalm bombs of '67

Watching hundreds of naked men
Ordered to kneel down blindfolded
In the carnage of destroyed streets
Stripped of their dignity
This enemy is insisting to relive
Days of Warsaw ghettos of WWII
Vengeance is their calling

The world can't seem to stop this 'moral army'
Till they are satisfied of spilling so much blood
Till they keep killing the children of the future

I can't seem to stop screaming

## Child of Gaza

I think of you day and night
I think of the brutality inflections
I think the enemy is never relenting

I am the child of Jerusalem
Reaching out to you
I was the child of Jericho
When the war came walking
To my sleepy town in 67'

I am the child of Haifa
Looking at the same sea
You are being slaughtered at
I think of you, day and night

I will return to Jericho
To sip mint tea
To smell the rain evaporating
In hot summer nights
Sleeping at my balcony

I don't know when you will return.

# Tariq Luthun

## The Summer My Cousin Went Missing

I should have asked how our *khalto* was holding
up, but I knew where she would be: her body

weary & unkind, buried in the day's tasks; back turned
to the home she grew up in; seeds in the

farm's soil, like miracles, sprouting as
she tends to them. Is this not always the case?

Child upon child goes, and someone's mother
is no longer a mother. My aunt – a mother herself – looks,

for a moment, away; nothing she plants has roots
long enough to hold. She turns back anyway, looks

ahead. If we are too caught up in the end – like boys
fleeing from the day's news – eyes worried

about that which we cannot control,
however will we stay fed? How-ever

will we live long enough to grieve?

# We Already Know This

*There is more to us than
what was taken from us.*
Quran


A place to call
home. Land of olive trees,
and their branches.
*Palestine*. There,
I've said it. I want to be sure
everyone knows where my parents
hail from. Each of us
needs a place to return to. Genocide,
I would hope everyone knows,
did not start, and did not end
at the Holocaust. I haven't forgotten that
everyone needs a place on this planet. And I,
I prefer to live where I can leave
the doors unlocked –
or live without the doors –
or hell. I don't even care
for walls. But I do care
for the blues: water, the sadness
that comes when it is not within
sight. I don't know if there is
a child, anywhere on this earth, that wasn't,
at least once, held by their mother. Water:
where my mother held me
until I was given to land. O firm land –
how my father holds me – people keep calling
for blood, to dress you in it.
I don't think any of them
know, truly, how much of it
the body can take; how much
the body can lose.

## Al-Bahr

I have seen death
look like me: bones sprawled
out somewhere between

hazel-coded grains along
the beach of the Red
Sea's shore – a palm opened and

a palm closed – body thick as
a fist in waning crimson tides.
Still, I've never known
a law to rewind a bullet

or a bomb, to unwind
a spine too busy wrapped
around Grief. I am told

we must learn to speak
with its tongue: too mired
in the end. I have seen this
all before: I watch men

who don't (and sometimes do) look like me
print tomorrow's face with our mothers'
graves. I'm incoherent

at this point, but I saw
a boy who could have become me
wash up on a shore.
Along another, I watched all

the boys lose a match. I guess
I'm not putting enough blame
on the child.

Don't get me
wrong. I'm just
wondering: can a boy
find death, and not

bring it home
to show everyone
what he's found?

# For Those We Left Behind

each day I ask my mother
what we do
              when we can't fight,
              and there is no money
left to give. tired, she raises
              her eyes from the dishes,
              her hands up from the bath,
and gives
              a gentle laugh,
              a sigh, *we make*
              *du'a, we pray*

              for whatever remains
     after the sea rises
to swallow our shore

# Sermon (For Those Who Survive)

If every day above ground is blessed,
then when will we sip a wine that does not flow

from the wounds hallowing our bellies? Where does this
vineyard lie, the one where our blood remains

just that? Every day, I crawl out of this cage,
elbows crimsoned & so fine; so aged with the sky's

knees in my back. My cries flutter & my throat loosens
to make space like a prison emptying its cells

into the earth below the earth. Now, here, I am
miles away & leagues above, watching

my cousins in the Holy Land drown in someone else's comfort;
another's desire for luxury. Cursed, I watch

the lexicon grow & grow. & god, I find
in every throne I lust;
       I shook
god in every breath I'd
hush. & whispered:

*I'm king*
       *so long as I'm able/*
*I'm good*
       *so long as I'm feared/*
*I'm full*
       *so long as I'm stable/*
*I'm prey*
*so long as I'm here.*

# I Go to the Backyard to Pick Mint Leaves for My Mother

Today, my mouth fell
wide when I saw the light
slip into the hills, and those boys

I grew up with did not
come back. Or, so I hear. Mama
would often ask me to gather

the mint leaves from behind our home,
and so, I would leave for this
nectar – without it, there is nothing sweet

to speak of. I pray that
when I am gone, my people speak
as sweetly of me as I do of them.

I see us, often, steeped
in the land and hope that
a shore remains

a shore – not a place to become
yesterday. The girls have joined the boys
now – all of them

tucked just beyond
the earth. But I know they wouldn't run
from their mothers – not without a fight,

a chase, a hunt, a honey, a home
for the tea to settle; a haven
for us to return to.

# Marwan Makhoul

## Portrait of the People of Gaza

The bitter ruins of Gaza
sprouted the arm of a child.
It waved at God two days ago
but the heavens were overcast
as their symbolic resonance had been rented to jets
to render that hand, pregnant with the phoenix
of the ashes, and so-called hope, unseen.
Last night I convinced myself to sleep
and not watch television.
I saw beyond the imagination of one dream-wounded.
There were dogs in Rafah
tasting pain.
There was our wounded childhood
begging a dog
'Kill me'
so feelings might have a reprieve from the jackboot.
Death, who sent you?
Who swept away the clouds of deepest winter,
so their
vultures could be seen circling the brink of life,
waiting to swoop down?
Death,
seek not the children,
depart.
They've gone on their own to the chilled compartments
        of the morgue.
All their loved ones are there, staying up late.

On the top floor, their mother Hasna
dies hurriedly
to stake a place in the graveyard for her little ones.
Death, who recommended me?
Death ...
How long have you been looking out for your children at school?
You know they're not there.
Didn't your enticing recklessness tell you it's a holy day?
Let me ask you ...
Where are the prophets of old
to deliver affliction from the guileless bullet?
The house next door has no room for salvation ...
I can see the unseen.
By the God who made grief a joke
before my eyes,
who made my assailant laugh at me?
Bewail the slaughtered my truce-seeking heart, and take note
of the calibre of the gun and the world's silence.
Forget atonement,
time and again you have slaughtered me tolerantly
and howled at nothing.
The Gospels are meaningless not wiping away the tears of the wounded
on the day the butcher flays my skin. So, I continue
in agony, the mystique having fallen away.
Merciful one, tell me
are you ignorant of the modern warmonger?
Do you equate the sword of tribesmen with the bomb?
By God, speak!
Has he who loves you won?
By God,
Answer!

## New Gaza

No time left
so don't linger in your mother's womb
my little boy hurry arrive
not because I long for you
but because war is raging
I fear you will not see
your country as I'd wish for you.

...

Your country is not soil
nor sea that foresaw our fate and died:
it is your people.
Come get to know it
before the bombs mutilate
and I am forced to gather the remains
for you to know that those gone were beautiful
and innocent.
That they had children just like you
they let escape
from the freezers for the dead
at every raid to skip as orphans
on a lifeline.

...

If you're late you may not
believe me and believe it is a land without a people
and that we were not really here at all.
Twice exiled, then we revolted
against our luck
for seventy-five years
once luck turned all bad
and hope turned grey.

...

The burden's too heavy
too much for you to bear
I know, forgive me for like a gazelle
giving birth I am afraid
of hyenas lying in wait to pounce behind
the pit. Come quick then run
as far as you can
so I'm not ravaged by regret.

...

Last night, despair exhausted me –
I said, keep quiet.
What's it to do with him?
My little one, child of the breeze,
what's the Storm to do with him?
But today I am compelled to come back
bearing breaking news:
they bombed the Baptist Hospital in Gaza,
among the 500 victims was a child
who calls to his brother, half his head blown off,
eyes open: 'My brother!
Can you see me?'
He does not see him
just as the frantic world
that condemned for two hours
then slept to forget him
and forget his brother,
does not see him.

...

What to tell you now?
Disaster and catastrophe are sisters
both ravenous and raging they attack me
until my lips tremble and from them drop
all possible synonyms for
corpse.
In time of war don't count on any poet
 they're as slow as tortoises
making futile efforts to race a massacre
that runs like a hare.
The tortoise creeps
and the hare leaps from crime to crime
as far as the Orthodox Church, now bombed
in the sight of God who's just come from
a mosque razed to dust they targeted
in the sanctuary of the saviour. Where is the saviour
when our Father who art in heaven actually is the airplane
one alone and with no partner
except the one on board who came to bomb us
but all he struck is our submission.
My child, on the cross now
there's enough room for all the prophets.
God knows all
but you and the innocent unborn like you
are yet to know.

# Hello Beit Hanoun

Hello!
Beit Hanoun?
I heard on the news
that an artisan baker has come
to distribute bread
on the back of fresh artillery,
and I also heard
that one of his loaves feeds
at least twenty children
and is so warm it burns, and solid
like a randomly targeted shell.
They said:
children woke up early that day
not to go to school
but to the local youth club
opposite the town's playground
that in summer is full enough for two massacres,
and a certain hope, the hope to live.
I also heard
that when they were on their way
they made light of their wounds
and poured blood on the corners
till blood took the colour of the streets
and feelings.
When I saw what I saw on the screen
I thought I was dreaming
or the TV was dreaming the impossible made real.
I never imagined, Beit Hanoun,
that you'd mean anything to me
what with all the fun I'm having
like being busy with friends discussing
whether wine in the bottle
ferments or not.

I never knew you'd mean anything to me,
even something small
something small, Beit Hanoun.
Hello...?
Hello...?
Beit Hanoun?
Can you hear me?
I think its phone's not working
or perhaps has gone to sleep,
it is very late, after all.
Never mind, let it go.
I've nothing better to do
than catch up with my brothers shading themselves
by the axed trunk of Arab solidarity.
Goodbye, Beit Hanoun.
Goodbye.

The homeland having fallen down a well
after sixty years, it's up to us
to raise the rope a little, then let it fall again,
for only thus will hope learn patience.

\*\*\*

My country is the rape victim
I will marry.

# Lines Without a Home

the closest people are those I love to ridicule
but never would
maybe because I worry for them
from the gloating of others

the whale thinks he's so big
but in the sea
he's tiny

dear sea, you really are great
you spit us out to our country
whenever we drown in its love

even so
when the river commits suicide in the sea
the fish long for fresh water

the day we die, the death living
within us will die

because the shadow is truly faithful
when we're put in the grave it no longer stands up
but sleeps next to us

my poems, you too will inevitably die
but still I will write
in the hope, albeit slim, that you will live
after me

*enough!*
death says to the tyrannical
*I'm full up*

in every death there is another life
but don't let your ideas run away with you
Mr Believer

what's this obsession?
I speak about death in all my poems
although its time will only really come
in the final poem

to be a '48 Palestinian means
being the strangest citizen in the world:
you beg all the world's states to protect you
from your state

every cloud has a silver lining:
in the light of the fire burning us
moths live at night

the problem of man: the justice he sees
others don't see
and vice versa

Salafism –
beautiful idea
but terrible when adopted by fools

apologies Ziad Rahbani:
hunger isn't a kafir
hunger is creative

despite the sun's action on the skin
the beggar's hand
stays pure white

in the past we opened the gates of Syria to gypsies
let them return the favour
and open their country to us, now we're migrant gypsies

a black crow in the snow is more beautiful
than every dove of peace
in the speeches of politicians

the flu has benefits
including gaining the sympathy
and concern of your family

excuse me, water,
when I pour you in a glass, I don't mean to trap you
in fact, I'm just like you
I want to live

why do we fear weapons
that do nothing
without us

sectarian, whenever the cross round your neck
gets bigger, it gets smaller inside you,
same with the crescent

we may not change the world with what we write
but we may shame it

they partitioned my homeland into two states
and it emigrated

hyenas don't assassinate hyenas
O mankind

onboard a boat in a gale
we strike the waves with the oars
so they calm down

after a long absence, I see you and shed tears
like after a long night the sun rises
and the ice weeps

even if westerners really robbed easterners
they would not be able to plunder
the sight of the sun shining

only before You
we aren't ashamed to take off our clothes
O God

in order for me to write poetry that isn't
political, I must listen to the birds
and in order to hear the birds
the warplanes must be silent

---

*Note: Ziad Rahbani is a Lebanese musician born in 1956. The song 'I'm not a kafir, hunger is a kafir' is from his 1985 album Ani Mish Kafir.*

# Mohammed Mousa

## In a country that doesn't need me, doesn't know my name, my skin colour, my favourite coffee, or even who I was

'What do you want to talk about?'
'I don't know! Hang on! Maybe I do know
but the view is a little bit disorientated.
Maybe, it is I who is disorientated, or maybe the sea.'
'Do you know how much I hate silence! Right! What do you mean the sea might be disorientated?'
'Silence! Can't you hear the noise around us? The songs, the cars, the voices of street vendors, the people around us? What silence are you talking about? The sea sometimes looks confused, tired, murky, and this has something to say about the hearts and eyes of those who look at it, those who have been in the sea or next to it, the sea is a witness to many things, ugly things and beautiful things, so it is normal to look disoriented, like we humans."
'Okay! I understand! I mean the silence between two people in a meeting, together. Two people who look alike. You see! Now we have something to talk about, I told you, I'm so good at breaking the ice.'
'There was no ice! Do you miss love?'
'I miss being in love, but I don't know if I miss love.'
'Have you ever been in love?'
'I have been in love with the remaining stars, the singing moon, the bold sunsets, the outdated city at night, and my new self.'
'I meant romantic love; but it's okay. You like to sound erudite, like ancient poets.'
'Do you believe in hope?'

'What? I do but it takes me to some places I don't want to go. Sometimes it creates unnecessary antagonisms for me with people I don't want to hurt.'
'Do you hate life?'
'Hate is a strong word, no, I love it, and I believe that life is meant to be lived, but I don't know how, I haven't reached that level of realisation yet."
''What do you believe in?'
'I believe in coffee at 6am and painting a fresh kiss on your dried lips at 2am, do you love coffee too?'
'I love tea, especially chamomile tea in midwinter, when the windows are closed – the clouds are welled up with tears, sound of rustling outside, rain washing the streets, and the warmth of the faint light in my room.'
'Sometimes I think about the women I haven't met, the women I was reluctant to speak to.'
'I think about the songs I haven't heard in the morning – and the movies I haven't watched in September.'
'I think about the conversations I haven't started – the faces I haven't seen, and the bodies whose presence I haven't felt.'
'What are you made of?'
'Mud, memories, wars, blood, and honey.'
'Are you lonely?'
'Yes, I am, I was never ashamed to confess it.'
'Where is your homeland?'
'I've lost it in a suitcase before I was born.'
'I feel extremely cold, cold enough to not think of those who failed me – those who closed the doors of life on me.'
'I watch my mottos falling out from my mouth and I can't even pick a few to let you know who I am and what I am trying to say.'
'Are you afraid?'
'Of what?'
'I don't know. Of anything.'
'I'm afraid and I'm not – the sky was loaded with bombs in May, this is terrifying.'
'Why have you left then?'
'Why wouldn't I?'

'Where do you want to go?
'I've left a place I know by heart to start a journey to somewhere whose name I don't even know.'
'Where?'
'In a country that doesn't need me, doesn't know my name, my skin colour, my favourite coffee, or even who I was.'

## Gaza children play in cemeteries

Gaza children are being killed in cemeteries.
If you ask the kids, they won't tell you
that they wanted to play amongst the dead.
They just thought they could play anywhere.
If you ask the dead, it may not matter if the children
intrude on their eternal slumber
when they trample
their sandy graves
with their bare feet.
It's not polite for the assassin
to attack the dead
while their graves are scorching on a summer's noon.
Gaza children always thought it was safe to play in a cemetery.
They thought
that there is no difference
between a cemetery and a playground,
and they played until
they tenanted the tombs in shreds.
Here on, there are no playgrounds for Gaza children
and cemeteries are always available.

# I don't want my memories to grow old on foreign soil

I want my memories
to be around me,
to resemble me, the colour of my dark skin,
and the brownness of my round eyes,
I want my memories
to speak a vernacular I speak,
to walk a lane I know.
I want them to ripen beneath a sky
that embraces me, that irrigates them,
when I am not there anymore.
If you ask me about my last plea,
it will be that my memories do not age away from me,
between the hearts of outsiders
who don't resemble me
or the hearts of those
who left them
roaming the streets alone
finding no
retreat.

I want them to age in their ancestral home
where there is some of me,
the chilliness of a newborn sea,
the flavour of oranges,
the lunchtime tea
under the almond tree,
the sweetness of my grandmother's cherries,
the Arabic coffee over the hills
that I am not allowed to see.
I don't want my memories to grow old
away from me.
I don't want my memories to grow old
in a foreign country.

## Salted Wounds

In Gaza we spray salt
on our fresh wounds,
on the placid skin of the dead,
on the feet of lovers,
in the eyes of absurd realities.
In Gaza salt heals,
our grandparents put salt
on their untouched cuts
but I wonder why salt doesn't heal
the soft skin of premature losses,
why my lesions are still so sharp
and very cold and why my pain is so brittle.
Why salt doesn't heal since I left.

# I can't keep up with the rhythm of war

I can't keep up with the rhythm of war, the ambulance sirens at the top of every hour and their nervous sound, the loud explosions and stun grenades before them during the hours of darkness. The quietude of sunbirds in the morning, the young man who digs up the graves of his murdered family and the tattered bodies throughout the city. The songs of the martyrs echoing through the tiny grey houses of northern Gaza, the unstoppable precautions of the newscaster. The broken accords at the crossroads at noon. The butchers at dusk and the hocks of young mothers. The unfulfilled fears developing in the heart of a brown-eyed girl, shrouded in the memory of losing her fiancé at the front.

I can't keep up with the rhythm of war, how the sky above the camp tears apart and falls on our heads at warp speed. We wash on the rubble, we breathe under the rubble, we fight death as we gasp and fight for a life that's ready to go.

## Three military vehicles drive by

Three military vehicles drive by old town in Gaza on Sundays
carrying soldiers who lost their identities to a stone
while our mothers finish a dinner for the little angels.
The dinner usually consists of cheese, thyme,
olive oil, fig jam and sage tea.
Two officers hide under the olive trees
in front of my room across the street,
ten soldiers with M16s, grenades, knives and maps.
Another military vehicle pulls up next to the house,
on their way to move
to a house on the outskirts of Gaza,
my house. As I dip bread in olive oil and Zaater,
I refuse to hand my body to a white soldier
who has no identity and asks me to leave for having one.

## Hungry Gaza Skies

Gaza,
As the bombs rain down on the city
like hellbats in the early hours,
in the presence of the gluttonous tanks,
I smoke alone on the roof,
watch the city turn crimson
while the fear of losing you rises again,
I wrap my little town in a carrier bag
and hide its people.
Still the moans of the young mother
reverberate in my head at 7am
while the announcer announces another
carnage in the North,
I hang my future bruise on the wall
then I twist my heart
and throw it into the famishing
heavens of Gaza.

# They ask me who I am

*A kid from the camp* I reply,
the largest refugee camp,
still they don't know but they
know well the boy who saved the fish
when his house was destroyed
from the largest open-air prison.

But why am I
explaining myself
to the one who put me in a camp,
inside a large prison
with open spaces
and tiny graveyards,
I am from the camp

and nothing I want more than a homeland,
unrestricted birthplace,
no fences of tyranny,
no walls of oppression,
no checkpoints to undress my fears,
with clouds heavy enough to carry my soul.

# Hiba Abu Nada

## We are in the heights now

teachers, free of their crowded classrooms,
their voices no longer shouting to be heard,
new families without pain or sadness,
journalists taking pictures of heaven
writing about the eternal love.
All, all of them are from Gaza.
There is a new Gaza in heaven
without siege
taking shape now.

# Good night, Gaza

Gaza's night is dark apart from the glow of rockets,
quiet apart from the sound of the bombs,
terrifying apart from the comfort of prayer,
black apart from the light of the martyrs.
Good night, Gaza.

# Naomi Shihab Nye

## Green Shirt

His mother did not wash it for this,
for him to be carried dead by two friends
across the thirsty ground of Gaza.

That morning he put it on, she told him
he looked handsome, a fine deep colour
that lit up his skin.

# Before I Was a Gazan

I was a boy
and my homework was missing,
paper with numbers on it,
stacked and lined,
I was looking for my piece of paper,
proud of this plus that, then multiplied,
not remembering if I had left it
on the table after showing to my uncle
or the shelf after combing my hair
but it was still somewhere
and I was going to find it and turn it in,
make my teacher happy,
make her say my name to the whole class,
before everything got subtracted
in a minute
even my uncle
even my teacher
even the best math student and his baby sister
who couldn't talk yet.
And now I would do anything
for a problem I could solve.

# Moon Over Gaza

I am lonely
for my friends.
They liked me,
trusted my coming.
I think they looked up at me
more than other people do.

I who have been staring down so long
see no reason for the sorrows humans make.
I dislike the scuffle and dust of bombs blasting
very much. It blocks my view.

A landscape of grieving
feels different afterwards.
Different sheen from a simple desert,
rubble of walls, silent children who once said
my name like a prayer.

Sometimes I am bigger than
a golden plate,
a giant coin,
and everyone gasps.

Maybe it is wrong
that I am so calm.

# Samah Sabawi

## Questions the media should ask the people of Gaza

How do you bury your dead when you're still running for cover?
How do you shelter from the bombs when they
        follow you like your shadow?
How do you dig through rubble in worn sandals and bare
        calloused hands?
How do you put together all the pieces of your loved ones?
Do you start with the head or the toe?
And do you always know where all the pieces go?

How do you operate on the wounded with no hospitals or anaesthetics?
How do you shelter at UN schools when they are bombed targets?
How do you cook with no food, no fuel, and no electricity?
How do you wash without taking your clothes off?
Are you that afraid of being pulled
From beneath the rubble naked?

How do you read to your little ones bedtime stories?
How do you shout them louder than the air strikes?
How do you calm night and day terrors?
How do you tell them monsters don't live under the bed?
        Or, in the closet.
                But that monsters now occupy the sky?

How do you explain why you write their names
        on their arms and legs?
How do you tell them you want their corpses to be recognized?
How do you worship after the bombing of your churches
        and mosques?
How do you still pray?
And how do you still believe
there is a God?

How do you drink contaminated water?
How do you share a toilet with fifty other families?
How do you go to sleep with eyes wide open?
How do you walk through massacres with eyes wide open?
How do you wish to die, so someone could close your eyes?
How do you say goodbye knowing it's the last time?
How do you breathe when every heartbeat aches?
How do you find a light in this long dark night?
How do you find courage when our world is cowardly?
How do you see with debris in your eyes more clearly
        than our heads of state?
How do you find faith?
How do you find hope?
How do you not give up on humanity?
How do you cultivate life
Every single day
Inside death's cradle?

# Sara M. Saleh

## Say Free Palestine

*a meditation after Sean Bonney*

*for 'I love you' say free Palestine,*
*for 'snooze the alarm' and 'snooze it again' say free Palestine,*
*for 'I need a drink, hold the ice' say free Palestine,*
*enter your 6-digit pin here, then say free Palestine,*
*for 'Are you seeing someone?' say free Palestine and for*
*anything 'pumpkin spice' say free Palestine,*
*for 'I'm freezing my <insert whatever body part here> off'*
*say free Palestine, for the* 'Great British Bake-Off *and* Love Island *and* The Bachelor'
*say free Palestine, for 'separation of church and state'*
*say free Palestine, for 'Twitter – I'm not calling that shit X'*
*say free Palestine,*
*for 'the limit does not exist' say free Palestine,*
*don't say 'rush hour' say free Palestine,*
*don't say 'Happy Birthday'*
*say free Palestine, definitely don't say 'Australia'*
*say Land Back and free Palestine, say 'sorry'*
*then say free Palestine*
*don't say 'humanitarian pause' say free Palestine,*
*maybe don't say 'there are two sides to this story'*
*don't say 'conflict' don't say 'collateral damage'*
*don't say 'eviction' don't say 'self-defence' –*
*just say free Palestine, say 'you are a demographic threat'*
*then say free Palestine, for 'bedtime lullabies',*
*sing Dammi Falastini then say free Palestine,*
        *say no justice, no peace,*
            *from the river to the sea, then say free Palestine.*

# The Business of Occupation Bingo

| B | I | N | G | O |
|---|---|---|---|---|
| Cycles of violence | Restore calm | Do you condemn? Do you condemn? Do you condemn? | Singling out Israel | Ancient religious conflict |
| Roadblock to peace | Palestinians die, Israelis killed | Israel vs Hamas war | Terrorists' | Hezbollah. Iran. IS*S... |
| Both sides | Human shields | Israel's right to self-defence | We must remain neutral | Collateral damage |
| Diplomatic negotiations | UN resolutions vetoed | Boycotts are antisemitic | Too complex | KhamasKhamasKhamasKhamasKhamasKhamasKhamas |
| Security threat | Humanitarian crisis | Israel is a haven for queer rights | US and Israel: mutual interests | Children of darkness |

# There are no colonisers in this poem

Only worshippers at al-Aqsa breaking their fast / in *i'tikāf* all night /
the *hakawati*'s stories flare through the Old City / in a crowd
of holiday wreaths and Christmas trees / which are trees and
not barbed wire / there are no colonisers in this poem / only
the old man / stringing and spiralling the cheesy *knafeh* / orange
blossom syrup caramelising his beard / another daughter returned
from exile / each arrival unclots his blood /
There are no colonisers in this poem / the snow
is unsentimental, the kids throw slush balls
at each other / there is no rush to get to class,
if they truant – it's their choice / they're just doing what
kids do / the frost-tipped tourists / exit the Austrian Hospice /
hot chocolates warming their mittens / There are
no colonisers in this poem / only lovers in the back
of cars / slipping out of towns and villages with no farewell
or fanfare / for a lick of the big city and their lover's
lips / there are no colonisers in this poem / sparrows
release their breaths in rhapsody / commuters start their morning
shifts / or sleep-ins / they can expect to make it wherever / there
are no colonisers in this poem / water unsullied / clean enough
to quench gardens and groves / sons join their mothers and
fathers / and grandparents for dinner / and arguments are just
arguments and not manifestos / there are no colonisers
in this poem / there is only wild joy / we are all here /

Shireen would be too.
And Roshdi. And Refaat. And Heba.

They would all be here, too.

# The Purging

When you reconstruct my jaw
handle with sensitivity,
it is in ruins.

You'll find my mouth open for the first time in a while,
for so long it has been a citadel. An unholy well.
A wail will come out,
don't be surprised if you happen upon other noises in there, too,
my father's praise, prayers for Gaza
nesting in my throat.
You may also detect the perfect English, the Arabic subtitles my mouth
could never accommodate,
and the taste of tears, clementines and cardamom in the hinges...

Baptise this mouth of the screams
and the indignities when they came for us.
Cleanse it of the abstinence, the ghosts of wedding vows
that were never recited.

As you rebuild, the words
may appear in anarchy.
Please, purge them from my mouth.
I don't ever want to see them again.

# Deema K. Shehabi

## Gaza Renga

From the underside of the bridge
to where the Mediterranean sutures the land,
one woman bronzes her arms,

someone's limbs
tucked into the lips

of her long dress.
She says, 'I saw the smoke.'
'It was not the smoke of a gardenless

earth nor the haemorrhage
of parentless children.'

   ***

This place is all we ever
grieve for –
in illegible dreams,

in passing hours,
the daylight sealed

from our eyes,
and nothing is ever limned:
a baby on top

of the mother's dried-up
corpse in broad daylight.

\*\*\*

The oil-stained boot prints
on the veil
are the same ones on the wall,

and the girl whose clothes
still smell like gas is replaced

by another with a rough voice
calling out... for what, to whom?
Balconies, buildings,

an ambulance with no driver
settle in the back of her throat.

# Light in the Orchard

The black crows don't rise frequently from yellow fields
in sunset anymore though the sentiment does – you see
the earth as a trammelled garment beneath your feet and
the blue, teeth-marked cavity of water and sky circling around,
blue on copper, blue-green, green-auburn, and although you
wish to repent and say: *no country is worth fighting for* – the rain
light will suddenly riffle through the breeze until finally you spot
the swans bristling on the pond,
blood-coloured clouds flaring in their black eyes,
and then away one last time to the orange grove,
where birds plight in your stall.

# Of Harvest and Flight

Beneath a wet harvest of stars in a Gaza sky,
my mother tells me how orchards
once hid the breach of fallen oranges,
and how during a glowing night

of beseeching God in prayer,
when the night nets every breath
of every prayer,
my uncle, a child then, took flight

from the roof of the house.
The vigilant earth had softened
just before his body fell to the ground,
but there's no succumbing to flight's abandon.

Our bodies keep falling on mattresses,
piles of them are laid out on living room floors
to sleep wedding visitors:
the men in their gowns

taunt roosters until dusk,
while women hold the stillness
with liquid harvest in their eyes,
and night spirits and soldiers

continue to stampede through the house
between midnight and three in the morning.
On the night of my uncle's nuptial,
I watch my mother as she passes

a tray of cigarettes to rows of radiant guests
with a fuchsia flower in her hair.
Years before this, I found a photograph
of her sitting on my father's lap,

slender legs swept beneath her,
like willow filaments in river light.
His arm was firm around her waist;
his eyes bristled, as though the years of his youth

were borders holding him back
and waiting to be scattered.
Those were the years when my mother
drew curtains tightly over windows

to shut out the frost of the Potomac;
she sifted through pieces of news
with her chest hunched over a radio,
as though each piece when found

became a space
for holding our endless
debris. But in truth,
it was only 1967, during the war,

three years before I was born.
Tonight, I'm old enough
to listen to a story told my mother
in Gaza beneath the stars.

I turn toward her after she's finished
to ask how a daughter
can possibly grow beyond
her mother's flight.

There's no answer;
instead she leans over me
and points to the old wall:
the unbolting of our roots *there*,

beside this bitter lemon tree,
and here was the crumbling
of the house of jasmine
arching over doorways,

the house of roosters
and child-flight legends,
this house of girls
with eyes of simmering seeds.

# Blue

'The breeze that came down from over the hills was no longer.'

Begin with your last gaze on the morning of your first departure,
your boyhood room in the haemorrhaging light, you are
      combing your hair and staring
out the window at the sunken city of Jaffa, *Bride of the Sea.*

There's a map composed on a white napkin that you hand to
      Donna and Omar:
walk six blocks back from the sea, the house later found behind a façade
of ancient sepia, and Donna says, 'This must be Tata's house.'

You say the sea will no longer cast its net on a city of vanished
inhabitants.

Before we cross the Allenby Bridge, you tell me about your first
leave-taking:

>'When we first arrived at the dock,
>the grey-blue waves were large hills
>
>that opened to a wide sky, the sea swallowing
>the small boat, the big boat beckoning,
>
>but the sea would not take
>us across to Lebanon that day; its secret voice
>
>kept crying out to me:
>*Freedom is land.*'

'Let's go to Nablus instead,' your sister Hind said, 'There's a house there...'

Big house full of cold, stone walls that break a person in half.

'Which half are you after so much disassembly?'

Begin again with the story of your children's mother:

> 'She rode that Tennessee Walking Horse regally
> at Little Daddy's Texas ranch, her back straight,
>
> her golden hair like an emissary of no known sun,
> her blue eyes unlike Mediterranean blue.
>
> I loved her since with all the darkness in my veins.
> Before I bought her a horse, I remembered how I sold cigarettes
>
> in the streets of Nablus. I bought Hind her first bra,
> and when I sold an entire carton, we ate lamb instead of vegetables.'

On the morning of your first departure, loudspeakers blared news of pregnant women with bayoneted bellies, and the dawn was no longer dawn, and the breeze was no longer.

'Does that man with the restaurant on the water still serve fried fish with lousy tahini?'

Omar sobs on the bus back to Jordan. The settlements rush toward him; from over the hills, he feels a choking. Donna says the blue of Palestinian pottery is unlike any blue she's ever seen.

# Dareen Tatour

## A moment before death

I will stay here
because the wounds in the land of Galilee
fill my emotions, they draw all my words to it.
For as long as I can keep singing, I will stay

because singing on the shore of Acre awakens my memory,
all the seagulls land on it,
because embraces, meetings and love
pour in on the country's breeze.

Because I love the unbearable
I will stay here, and ride the high wind
that refuses to submit to the oppressors.
I will stay
because the paths in my country,
despite the bleeding,
awaken my feelings of life
and bleed with oppression like mine.

I will stay
because the children here know
the answer as well as I do:
If you ask the small child,
'Tell me what you will dream about at night?'
he looks long at the sky,
he listens to the roar of missiles for so long,
he answers so sadly: 'Why am I thinking about this matter
when I may not live until the evening?
I won't survive for long,
the bullets will fly any moment.'

Whatever I want and what I could hope for are here
and here I may live, here I may die
and with all this.
I will stay here loving life,
I will stay to write about myself
and everyone who suffers the language of truth
because writing in war is a quick death,
it contains victory and sacrifice.
I will write from the darkness of the caves,
perhaps I will greet the sunrise
because poetry is like the tip of a sword,
like the thunder of the sky.
All the bullets they fire to silence language,
to kill our memory, to kill
what is old and what is new
for the sake of genocide
will stoke our resilience and our will
and therein will be salvation.

# The general, my brother and me

O General,
Instruct / teach your soldiers to apologize
for the essence / meaning of childhood
and to the spirit of innocence

O General,
You must apologize
for tampering with the colour of the sky,
the colour of the air,
the colour of the seas,
which you turned into the colour of blood.

\*\*\*

Oh, my brother in the sense
do not weaken
we have what remains for us of tears
they bequeathed to you as they bequeathed to me the tents of exile
they have dressed you as they have dressed me in the clothes of
        torment, and all the tragedies
Oh, my brother in Gaza
the killer of my mother and your mother
they are the same on the map of history

\*\*\*

Oh my brother in fact
I fight with the letter and with the poem
So that love is not put at the mercy of the general
To bring roses to my sad city
So that the cloud above us does not turn into a shell
I resist with the letter and with the poem
So as not to mess with the shape of the field, the colour of the
    sky, the waves of the sea, and the light of day
So as not to change the shape of the plains, the colour of the sky,
    the waves of the seas, and the light of the day
so that Zaatar remains in the ground

## The child and the sea

O sea
I am the child
I am a refugee to you from death and war, from shells and killing...
I call out, with a wish in my voice, asking for mercy...
I hope to return to the homeland from deprivation.

O sea,
I am the child
tell me,
my breath didn't move that soldier to declare his victory by bombing my house and turning my body into pieces?

# When Gaza was killed

The poem emigrated, and with it the melody and the song;
war brought wounds, pain and medicines,
we live our lives, our nights and our days, in a prison
and in a graveyard;
weddings die, funerals take place;
there is nothing new in the news
other than the lack of bread,
other than the scarcity of shrouds, bed and cover, other than the killing of wishes,
other than the fight and flight and control;
every day here is a funeral, bombs, and a massacre,

none could see this epic as anything else,
tens of thousands have died
a country is lost
and the diaspora on the borders as tents line up
my people still say: either martyrdom or steadfastness,
freedom then life

# I will not die

I will keep dreaming as long as I live
as I long as I want
this is how I live
the dead are those who do not dream
I will not stop my dreams... No
I am staying
I will not die

# Mosab Abu Toha

## What is Home?

What is home:

it is the shade of trees on my way to school
before they were uprooted.

It is my grandparents' black-and-white wedding photo
before the walls crumbled.

It is my uncle's prayer rug,
where dozens of ants slept on wintry nights,
        before it was looted and put in a museum.

It is the oven my mother used to bake bread and roast chicken
before a bomb reduced our house to ashes.

It is the café where I watched football matches and played –

My child stops me: Can a four-letter word hold all of these?

# Lena Khalaf Tuffaha

## Grisaille

The method is simple
and civilized. A canvas must be stripped
then prepared, the scale of shadows
and highlights defined, a foundation
of values laid out upon which
the victor's colours will be saturated.

Our children learn the maps
of homeland in war time
on screens emblazoned with their cousins' limbs,
vermillion streaks across the gaping
craters of their levelled neighbourhoods.

It is said this technique comes from Europe.
It is said the soldiers are livid
for being forced to kill
it is said *disperse them*

Our children study these images,
their cousins' corpses lightfast,
their cries passing through
networks of metal and verdigris,
calling for water and father and air.

It is said, more succinctly, *flatten it all*
it is possible for the light
to be reflected back to the viewer
for the effect of luminosity.

# Pianissimo

If you say it softly/if you linger in the vowels/there is precedent/ in tajweed the tradition/ is incantatory/even though you don't/call it song/if you count/six beats for every long /alef/like lifting a prayer up to the sky/like hoisting a body above the ruins/and the arms raised up in praise/in grieving/praise/if you choose/a softer word here/read a poem about/ love instead/ if you add the word/if you loosen the grip/if you say it/ in Arabic/say it in Arabic/in Arabic whisper/choose the one that rhymes/even if /it is reserved for the dead/if you sing/sing it a little/the crowd begging/the sky/begging the collapsed/begging the earth to stop caving in/ blessing the baby delivered/again/from the rubble /beseeching the walls/the crowd passing the newborn hand over hand over/heads garlanded in concrete dust/Allahu Akbar always/translated as indictment/instead say/something/ soft/stretch the syllables/let us hear

# The State of –

Noun gerund of the verb (to journey)
A setting out, a departure
A boy's voice calls out from beneath what used to be
the second story of a house
*I am here* he cries *can anyone hear me?*
*I am here and the night sky is sleeping on my chest*

Noun gerund of the verb (to leave)
An exodus, a detachment
A father has gone in search of bread
A baker has gone in search of flour
A mother has gone in search of a cloud
A people have gone
A world in each of them

Noun gerund of the verb (to travel)
A parting, a demise
A girl steps on top of the walls of what used to be
the third story of a house
*I am searching for the sea* she cries
*Has anyone seen it? It used to live in my window.*

# Abjadarian* in Autumn

*Atmospheric river* the meteorologists warn,
inches swell and flood in hours. In the surge, leaves
undulate, severed from ash and poplar,
      from the mammoth cottonwoods.

Bereft of colour, I study the redbud's last holdout.
Tremulous. Defiant, as the rain batters the trees.
Thickets of fallen neighbours at the base of the redbud

jeer loudly from the leaf's future, their russet veins strafed in mud.

حكاية موسمية رقصة الرياح مع الشجر

خاتمتها اغصان عارية تحتضن اعشاشا مهجرة

Day by day, the light slips through our fingers,
the bulldozer's jaws are insatiable. Rosemary and

red clay and stone. A family again buries their son's limbs.
Zealotry wears a custom-made suit, tweets about libel. Time is now

saturated with the melancholy of repetition, spiralling descent,
shopworn incredulities. It all reads like memory generated by
      algorithm,

صلينا مليا على الشهداء و لكن قبورهم راحت

حية نهج المحادثات

طالبوا بالبقاء كما اعتاد الاحياء منا ان نفعل

ظنوا بانهم نالوا حق الصخور التي

عانقت اجسادها الارض و سكنتها لكنهم

غفلوا حقدا لا ينهكه الزمن

Familiar platitudes clutter the timeline
قوت امواتنا دعاء الأمهات المتعبة وأمطار تشرين

Quiet reigns. From inside, the rain is soundless, the trees
keening, glimmering. Eventually, the redbud

loosens its grip and I am not there to witness, the letting go

matter-of-fact, the metaphor monstrous.

No need for such melodrama, there is actual suffering to attend to,

how it unfolds, how I unfold it by withholding my anger, or by

wasting it where it cannot be of use, commemorating massacres from

yesterday while tomorrow's eddy and flow.

---

*Note: Abjadarian is a form that speaks to its Abcedarian cousin but follows the order of the Arabic alphabet and refuses to settle for alternatives to letters and sounds for which English has no capacity*

# Acknowledgements

### Refaat Alareer
'If I must die' was subsequently shared worldwide on social media and translated into over 40 languages. 'I Am You' was originally published on *Mondoweiss* (mondoweiss.net, 2012) has also been published widely published online at Reddit, Instagram etc. since his death.

### Hala Alyan
'Naturalised' was first published in *Jewish Currents*, 20 October 2023, and 'I don't mean to hate the sparrows' in *Guernica Magazine*, 6 November 2023.

### Farid Bitar
'Unexplained misery', 'The Journalist', 'Child of 'Gaza' all appear in *Testament / Sajél* (Culture Matters, 2024). 'Unexplained misery' was first published on *The Recusant*.

### Tariq Luthun
During the 2023 Gaza war, the final four lines from his poem 'Lines Without a Home' became a slogan raised by tens of millions of protestors and written on the walls of cities around the world in the call for an end to the targeting of civilians.

### Hiba Abu Nada
'We are in the heights now' is translated from the Arabic by Atef Alshaer. 'Goodnight Gaza' previously appeared untitled on X and at *Literary Hub* lithub.com.

### Naomi Shihab Nye
'Green Shirt' previously appeared in *Tikkun*, 'Before I was a Gazan' in *Voices in the Air* (Greenwillow Books/ Harper Collins), and 'Moon Over Gaza' in her collection *The Tiny Journalist* (BOA Editions).

**Sarah M. Saleh**
'There are no colonisers in this poem' and 'The Purging' are from Saleh's debut poetry collection, *The Flirtation of Girls/ Ghazal el-Banat* (UQP, 2023).

**Deema K. Shehabi**
'Gaza Renga' first appeared in *Letters to Palestine*, edited by Vijay Prashad. 'Light in the Orchard', 'Of Harvest and Flight' and 'Blue' first appeared in her full-length collection of poems, *Thirteen Departures from the Moon*, published by Press 53.

**Dareen Tatour**
These poems have previously been published in the Swedish journal *Prevance.*

**Mosab Abu Toha**
'What Is Home?' previously appeared in the *Morning Star* 32 November 2023.

**Lena Khalaf Tuffaha**
The Arabic script in 'Abjadarian in Autumn' is translated by Atef Alshaer.

# Biographies

**Ali Abukhattab** is a poet, critic, translator and researcher in the fields of philosophy, religion and politics. He was born in Gaza City, and studied English literature and translation at the Al Zaytoonah University of Jordan. He lives in Norway. He has published books, contributed to various anthologies and published many critical papers and political and cultural articles. He has also written books for children. He has participated as a lecturer in cultural events, and as a political analyst on TV programmes. He is co-founder of 'Utopia' commune which has held many literary and intellectual events in the Gaza strip. Because of threats from the Hamas movement, he escaped to Egypt where he participated in the cultural life of Cairo. The International Cities of Refuge Network (ICORN) helped him move to Molde in Norway where he still lives in exile. He is guest writer for both ICORN and Norwegian PEN.

**Refaat Alareer** Ph.D. (1979–2023) was a Palestinian writer, poet, professor, and activist from the Gaza Strip. He was born in Gaza City and studied at the Islamic University of Gaza, University College London, and the Universiti Putra Malaysia. He was editor of *Gaza Writes Back: Short Stories from Young Writers in Gaza, Palestine* (2014), and *Gaza Unsilenced* (2015), and published numerous essays on life under occupation. On 6 December 2023 he was assassinated along with his family when the IDF 'surgically bombed' his apartment. His poem 'If I must die' was subsequently shared worldwide on social media and translated into over 40 languages.

**Hala Alyan** is a Palestinian American writer and clinical psychologist whose work has appeared in *The New Yorker, The New York Times, POETRY*, and elsewhere. Her poetry collections have won the Arab American Book Award and the Crab Orchard Series, and her debut novel, *Salt Houses*, won the Dayton Literary

Peace Prize. Her latest novel, *The Arsonists' City*, was a finalist for the 2022 Aspen Words Literary Prize. Her forthcoming collection of poetry, *The Moon That Turns You Back*, will be published by Ecco. Website: www.halaalyan.com

**Farid Bitar** is a Palestinian-American poet and painter, born in Jerusalem in 1961. In 1996, he translated, transliterated and edited *A Treasury of Arabic Love* (Hippocrene Books). He has published two books of poetry, *Footprints in the Mist* (iUniverse Books, 2011), and *Screaming Olives* (Smokestack Books, 2021). His poems are included in *A Blade of Grass: New Palestinian Poetry* (Smokestack Book, 2017) His third collection, *Testament / Sajél* is forthcoming from Culture Matters.

**Tariq Luthun** is a Detroit-born, Dearborn-raised community organizer, data consultant, and Emmy Award-winning poet. The son of Palestinian Muslim immigrants from Gaza, he is a Kresge Arts in Detroit fellow that earned his MFA in Poetry from the Program for Writers at Warren Wilson College. Luthun's work has earned him Best of the Net, in addition to fellowships through Kundiman, The Watering Hole, and the Kresge Foundation. His work has appeared in *Vinyl Poetry, Lit Hub, Mizna*, and *Button Poetry*, among others. He also serves as a board member for The Offing Literary Magazine. Luthun's first collection of poetry, *How the Water Holds Me*, was awarded Editors' Selection by Bull City. He won an Emmy Award for his production with the University of Michigan Health Systems, and has been nominated for a Pushcart Prize, Bettering American Poetry, and Best New Poets.

**Marwan Makhoul** is a Palestinian poet, born in 1979 in the village of al-Buqei'a, Upper Galilee, to a Palestinian father and a Lebanese mother. He works in engineering as a managing director of a construction company. He has several published works in poetry, prose and drama, including the poetry collections: *Hunter of Daffodils, Land of the Sad Passiflora, Verses the Poems Forgot with Me, Where Is My Mom*, and *A Letter from the Last Man*. For his first play, *This Isn't Noah's Ark*, won the best playwright award at

The Acre Theatre Festival in 2009. His poetry is also award winning and has appeared worldwide in Arabic publications. Several of his poems have been set to music. Selections from his poetry have been translated into English, Turkish, Italian, German, French, Hebrew, Irish, Serbian, Hindi, Polish, Dutch, Albanian, Macedonian, Portuguese, Amharic, Eastern Armenian, Bangla, Hindi, Telugu, Tamil, Malayalam, Marathi, Russian, and Urdu.

**Mohammed Mousa** is a Palestinian poet and journalist who was one of three writers shortlisted for the 2022 international Freedom of Expression Awards presented by the Index on Censorship. Born in Gaza, he grew up in the Jabalia refugee camp, studied English at college, and began his career as a translator for international journalists in 2014. In 2018 he created the Gaza Poets Society as a forum for young Palestinians to share their work in English and Arabic. His first collection, *Flamingo*, was published by the Gaza Poets Society, and his latest, *Salted Wounds*, by the Scottish-based publisher Drunk Muse Press in 2023. He was awarded the Times Richard Beeston Bursary in 2019 and completed his fellowship in London in 2022. His mother, father, two sisters and their grandsons were killed in the Jabalia camp. His father was a driver for the Red Crescent.

**Hiba Abu Nada (1991–2023)** was a Palestinian poet, novelist. She was born in Mecca, Saudi Arabia to a family of Palestinian refugees displaced by the depopulation of the village of Bayt Jirja by Israeli forces during the first Nakba. A graduate of the Islamic University, Gaza and Al-Azhar University, she worked at the Rusul Centre for Creativity, associated with the al-Amal Institute for Orphans. She published a number of collections of poetry, and a novel, *Oxygen is not for the Dead,* which won second place in the 20th annual Sharjah Award for Arab Creativity 2017. On 20 October 2023, she was killed by an Israeli airstrike while at her home in Khan Yunis in southern Gaza. She was 32.

**Naomi Shihab Nye** is a Palestinian-American writer, editor and educator. She grew up in St. Louis, Jerusalem, and San Antonio, Texas, where she graduated from Trinity University and continues to live. She has been Young People's Poet Laureate for the US (Poetry Foundation), poetry editor for the *New York Times* magazine and *The Texas Observer*, and a visiting writer in hundreds of schools and communities all over the world. Her books include *Everything Comes Next, The Tiny Journalist, Voices in the Air, Sitti's Secrets, Habibi, This Same Sky,* and *The Tree is Older than You Are: Poems & Paintings from Mexico*. Her volume *19 Varieties of Gazelle: Poems of the Middle East* was a finalist for the National Book Award. *The Turtle of Oman* and *The Turtle of Michigan* have both been part of the Little Read program, North Carolina. She has received Lifetime Achievement Awards from The Texas Institute of Letters, the Arab American National Museum, and the National Book Critics Circle.

**Samah Sabawi** is a playwright, author and poet. Her recent critically acclaimed play *THEM* won a Green Room Award for Best Writing, was shortlisted for the Nick Enright Prize for Playwriting and the Victorian Premiere Literary Awards, and was selected for the Victorian Certificate of Education playlist. Sabawi's play *Tales of a City by the Sea* has had more than 100 performances around the world, and won two Drama Victoria Awards. Sabawi is co-editor of *Double Exposure: Plays of the Jewish and Palestinian Diasporas*, winner of the Patrick O'Neill Award and co-author of *I Remember My Name: Poetry by Samah Sabawi, Ramzy Baroud and Jehan Bseiso*, and winner of the Palestine Book Award. Sabawi is currently working with Outer Urban Theatre Projects on the stage collaboration *Vigil*, finishing her debut novel *Cactus Pears for my Beloved*, to be published by Penguin Random House, and producing her first animation feature, *How We Fall in Love*. Sabawi was awarded a PhD at Victoria University and is the founder and director of Hakawatieh Productions.

**Sara M. Saleh** is a writer/poet, human rights lawyer, and the daughter of Palestinian, Lebanese and Egyptian migrants. Her poems, essays and short stories have been published widely in English and Arabic. Her first novel, *Songs for the Dead and the Living* (Affirm Press), and first full-length poetry collection, *The Flirtation of Girls/Ghazal el-Banat* (UQP) were both released late 2023. She won both the 2021 Peter Porter Poetry Prize and the 2020 Judith Wright Poetry Prize, was recently shortlisted for the University of Canberra's Vice-Chancellor's Prize, is the recipient of the inaugural Affirm fellowship for Sweatshop writers, a Neilma Sidney travel grant, Varuna writer's residency, and Amant writer's residency in New York, amongst other honours. She is based on Bidjigal land (Sydney, Australia) with her partner and their four cats.

**Deema K. Shehabi** is a Palestinian poet, writer, and editor. She is the author of *Thirteen Departures from the Moon* and co-editor with Beau Beausoleil of *Al-Mutanabbi Street Starts Here*, for which she received a Northern California Book Award. She is also co-author of *Diaspo/Renga* with Marilyn Hacker and winner of the Nazim Hikmet poetry competition in 2018.

**Dareen Tatour** is a Palestinian poet, photographer, filmmaking, political activist, and social media activist from Reineh, Palestine. Tatour is the recipient of the OXFAM Novib/PEN award 2019 for freedom of expression. A Hebrew online magazine, *Maayan*, awarded Tatour the 2016 prize for creativity in struggle. In 2017 she was awarded Danish Carl Scharenberg Prize for standing against injustice through poetry. In 2020 she won the Freedom of Expression Award in Oslo, Norway. In 2015, Tatour published a poem on YouTube and Facebook titled 'Qawem Ya Shaabi Qawemahum' ('Resist my people, resist them'), which led to her arrest and indictment. A full translation of the poem as made by a police officer is cited in the indictment document. She was sentenced to five months in prison after serving three years in house arrest. Publications: *The Last Invasion* (El Wattan Books, 2010), *My Threatening Poem* (Dyar Publishing, 2018), and three collections with Drunk Muse Press: *Threatening Poem – Memoir of a Poet in Occupation Prisons* (2020), *I Sing from the Window of Exile* (2023), *A Balcony Over a City Engulfed by War* (2023). She has had two plays performed: *I, Dareen Tatour* (in collaboration with Einat Weitzman, dir. Nitzan Cohen, 2018), and *Min Hotfulla Dikt* (Sweden, 2022). Other awards: ICORN residency in Sweden, 2023: the Palestine Book Awards 2023 for *I Sing from the Window of Exile*.

**Mosab Abu Toha** is a Palestinian poet, scholar, and librarian from the Gaza Strip. He was born in 1992 in the Al-Shati refugee camp, shortly before the signing of the Oslo Accords. He graduated in English from the Islamic University of Gaza. In 2017, he founded the Edward Said Library, an English language public library in Beit Lahia, of which a second branch was opened in Gaza City in 2019. In 2023, he earned an MFA in Poetry from Syracuse University in the United States. He taught English at United Nations Relief and Works Agency (UNRWA) schools in Gaza from 2016 until 2019, and is the founder of the Edward Said Library, the only English-language library in Gaza. In 2019–20 he was a visitor at Harvard University, as a Scholar-at-Risk Fellow at the Department of Comparative Literature, a librarian at the Houghton Library, and a fellow in the Harvard Divinity School. He is a columnist for *Arrowsmith Press*, and has written from Gaza for *The Nation, Literary Hub* and the *New York Times* and *The New Yorker*. His poems have been published in *Poetry Magazine, Banipal, Solstice, The Markaz Review, The New Arab, Peripheries, The New York Review, The Progressive, The New Yorker*, and *The Atlantic*. His debut poetry collection *Things You May Find Hidden in My Ear* (City Lights, 2022) won the Palestine Book Award and an American Book Award. It was also a finalist for the National Book Critics Circle Award and the Walcott Poetry Prize. In November 2023, while heading to the Rafah border, Toha was detained by the IDF. He was subsequently released following international pressure from PEN America and PEN International. He is now in Cairo, Egypt with his family.

**Lena Khalaf Tuffaha** is a poet, essayist, and translator. She is the author of three books of poems, *Water & Salt,* winner of the 2018 Washington State Book Award, *Kaan and Her Sisters* (Trio House, 2023), and *Something About Living,* winner of the 2022 Akron Prize, forthcoming from University of Akron Press in 2024. Tuffaha served as the translator and editor for *the Baffler* magazine's series *Poems from Palestine, 2022.*